ACTION SCIENCE

MAKING THINGS MOVE

Neil Ardley

Series consultant: Professor Eric Laithwaite

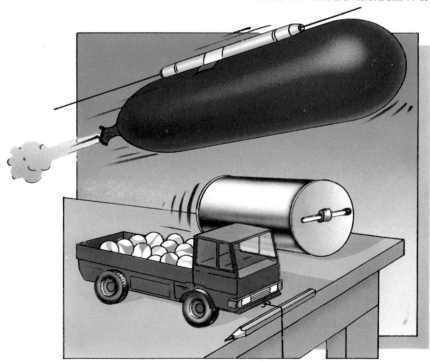

Franklin Watts

London   New York   Toronto   Sydney

The author
Neil Ardley gained a degree in science and worked as a research chemist and patent agent before entering publishing. He is now a full-time writer and is the author of more than fifty information books on science, natural history and music.

The consultant
Eric Laithwaite is Professor of Heavy Electrical Engineering at Imperial College, London. A well-known television personality and broadcaster, he is best known for his inventions on linear motors.

© 1984 Franklin Watts Ltd

First published in Great Britain in 1984 by Franklin Watts Ltd 12a Golden Square London W1

First published in the United States of America by Franklin Watts Inc. 387 Park Avenue South New York N.Y. 10016

Printed in Belgium

UK edition:
ISBN 0 86313 081 X
US edition:
ISBN 0-531-03771-1
Library of Congress Catalog Card Number: 83-50854

Designed by
David Jefferis

Illustrated by Janos Marffy, Hayward Art Group and Arthur Tims

MAKING THINGS MOVE

Contents

Equipment

In addition to a few everyday items, you will need the following equipment to carry out all the activities in this book.

Ball bearing	Gyroscope	Straws
Balloons	Magnet	Thin strong thread
Bicycle wheel	Plastic tube	Toy truck
Big button	Playing card	Two identical eggs
Cotton spool	Revolving chair	Weights
Empty detergent bottle	Stopwatch	

Introduction

As a baby, you were fascinated by movement. First you watched with darting eyes as people moved around you, then you delighted in pushing and dropping any object you could grasp, and finally you learned to move yourself. So you joined a world that is ever on the move in a turmoil of natural and manmade movements.

Movement is a form of energy, and it is produced by the action of force. By doing the activities in this book, you will find out how force and the energy in movement can bring about all kinds of motion, and why things move in various ways. You'll also explore the effects of movement, such as the strange properties of circular motion.

As you move through this book— whirling, firing, dropping, rolling, spinning, pushing, pulling, tipping, swinging, colliding (and playing some tricks)—spare a thought for safety and please don't behave dangerously.

✴ This symbol appears throughout the book. It shows you where to find the scientific explanation for the results of an experiment.

Getting going

Force gets things moving, then they keep on going until force acts again.

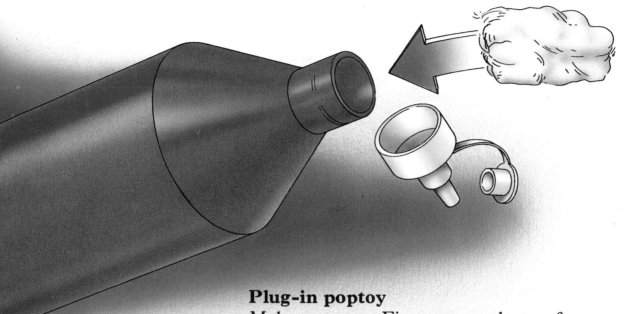

△ Make the plug by wetting some tissue paper and rolling it between your fingers.

Plug-in poptoy
Make a poptoy. First remove the top from an empty plastic detergent bottle. Then make a plug of tissue paper and push it into the top of the bottle. Now squeeze the bottle hard. The plug flies out with a pop and may travel a long way before falling to the ground.

✺ As you squeeze the bottle, you compress the air inside and the air builds up in pressure. The air pushes on the plug with increasing force. When the force is great enough, the plug is pushed out of the bottle and starts moving. Once it has left the bottle, the plug gets no more force from the compressed air. It keeps moving without any forward force. However, another force—gravity—pulls it down to the ground.

Invisible action

Roll a ball bearing across a smooth, flat table top. Watch how it moves in a straight line once it has left your hand. Now place a strong magnet on or under the table and roll the bearing near it. As it approaches the magnet, the bearing suddenly swerves.

Once a force has set an object moving, it continues to move at the same speed in a straight line unless another force acts on it. Gravity cannot pull the ball bearing, so it rolls in a straight line over the table. But when the invisible force of the magnet acts on the bearing, it makes it change direction and speed.

△ The harder you can squeeze the bottle, the faster the plug will move.

▽ If the tabletop is not very flat, it may help to roll the ball bearing along the edge of a ruler.

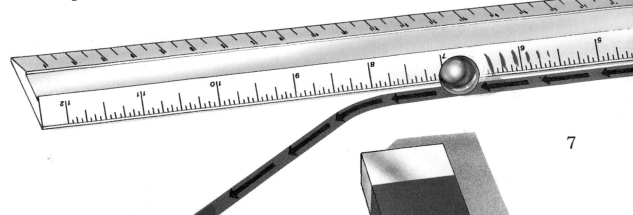

7

Gravity and its grip

See how the force of gravity acts equally on everything, no matter how big or how small.

△ One person must check that the weight is dropped at exactly the same moment that the tennis ball leaves the table. They will land together, no matter how far the tennis ball goes.

Over the edge

One person stands by the edge of a table, holding a weight at the level of the table. Another rolls a tennis ball along the table. If the first person drops the weight as the tennis ball leaves the table, they will both hit the floor at the same time.

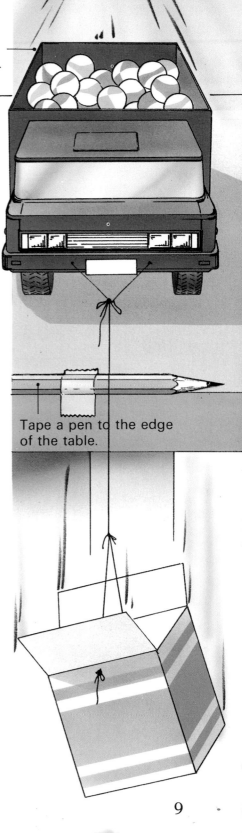

Friction will stop the truck if you overload it.

☀ The tennis ball begins to fall towards the floor at exactly the same moment as the weight. Gravity is the only force that acts on them, and it pulls the ball and the weight down equally. As they both fall downwards the same distance, they take exactly the same time and hit the ground together.

Show of force
Cut a cardboard carton in half and fasten it to a toy truck by a piece of string about a yard long. Place the truck on a smooth tabletop and let the carton hang over the edge. Put various numbers of weights or marbles in both the carton and truck, and time how long it takes the truck to move along the table. The time, and therefore the speed, depends on the weights of the carton and the truck.

Tape a pen to the edge of the table.

☀ The speed that any moving object reaches depends on the force acting on it, how heavy it is and for how long the force acts. The force of gravity pulls the carton, which in turn pulls the truck. The force on the truck is greater if the carton is heavier, making it move faster. But the speed of the truck also depends on how heavy it is. The heavier it is, the slower it moves.

Continued *overleaf*

9

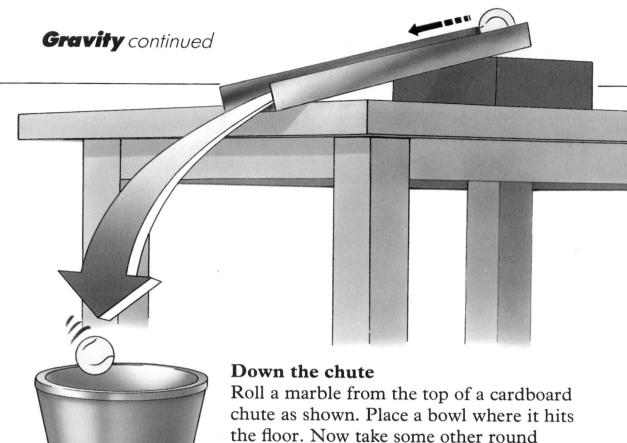

△ Each ball lands in the same place, so you don't need to move the bowl. This is because gravity makes both light and heavy objects fall at the same speed.

Down the chute

Roll a marble from the top of a cardboard chute as shown. Place a bowl where it hits the floor. Now take some other round things, like a tennis ball, an orange, a ball bearing and a little silver ball used for cake decoration. Roll each one from the top of the chute, but first ask a friend to place the bowl where it will land.

The force of gravity moves each ball down the chute and into the bowl. The bigger the ball, the greater the force on it. But because the bigger ball weighs more, the greater force does not make it move faster than a light ball. Gravity therefore acts equally on every ball, making them all move in the same way so that they land in the same place.

The force of friction

Friction opposes motion. Find out ways of using it as well as reducing it.

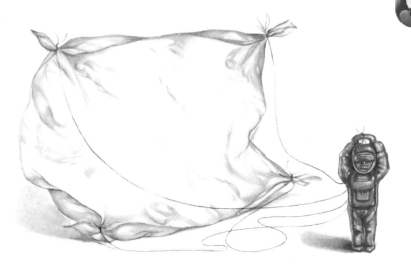

Taming gravity

Make a parachute from a large square of polythene. Tie a length of string about 20 in long to each of the four corners. Then knot the four pieces of string together and fasten a weight to the knot. Throw the whole parachute into the air, and it will float slowly back to the ground.

As gravity pulls it to the ground, air pushes against the parachute because it is large. The force produced by the air is called friction. It opposes the force of gravity, so the parachute falls slowly.

△ Parachutists can control their descent by using cords to vary the air flow in the parachute.

Continued overleaf

Column of coins

Place a column of coins, preferably of the same size, on a smooth surface such as a tabletop. Challenge your friends to move the whole column just by touching the top coin. The column always falls over—until you do it. The trick is to press down very hard on the nearest edge of the top coin; then the whole column moves.

▽ Try this trick out on your own first to find how many coins you need. This will depend on the smoothness of the surface. This trick works because the friction between smooth surfaces is always less than it is between rough ones.

When you press on the coins, friction increases between them and stops them moving apart. But there is less friction between the bottom coin and the smooth surface, so the whole column moves.

4 in

Pinhole in middle of card

Model hovercraft

Cut out a circle of stiff card about 4 in across and make a small hole in the middle with a drawing pin. Now find a tube wide enough for the neck of a balloon to fit tightly over it. Glue a section of the tube about 2 in long over the hole in the card. Then blow up the balloon and, keeping it inflated, fit the neck over the tube. Place the card on a smooth tabletop, and it floats like a hovercraft.

The air that comes out of the balloon spreads out beneath the card, lifting it just above the surface. Because the card and tabletop hardly touch, there is very little friction between them and the card moves easily.

△ Take great care not to bend the card. It must be completely flat.

▽ A hovercraft forces air beneath its hull to float over the water.

Action and reaction

Find out that whenever a force acts, so does another force.

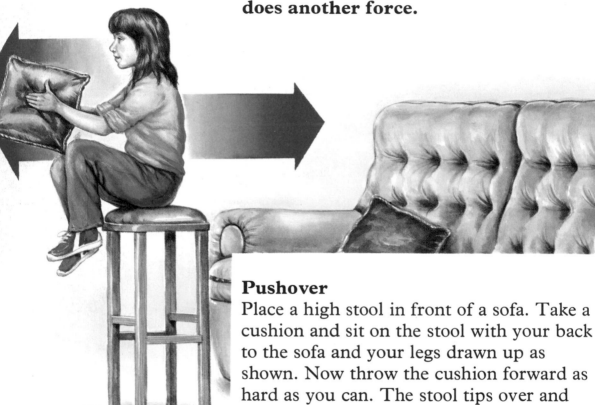

Pushover

Place a high stool in front of a sofa. Take a cushion and sit on the stool with your back to the sofa and your legs drawn up as shown. Now throw the cushion forward as hard as you can. The stool tips over and you fall back into the sofa.

✳ As you exert a force on the cushion and throw it forward, the cushion exerts a force on you and pushes you backward. The first force is called the action and the second the reaction. Whenever any force is applied, an equal reaction force is always produced in the opposite direction.

△ Normally, you don't notice the reaction that accompanies a force. Here it is enough to push you over because you are sitting high up on a narrow stool.

14

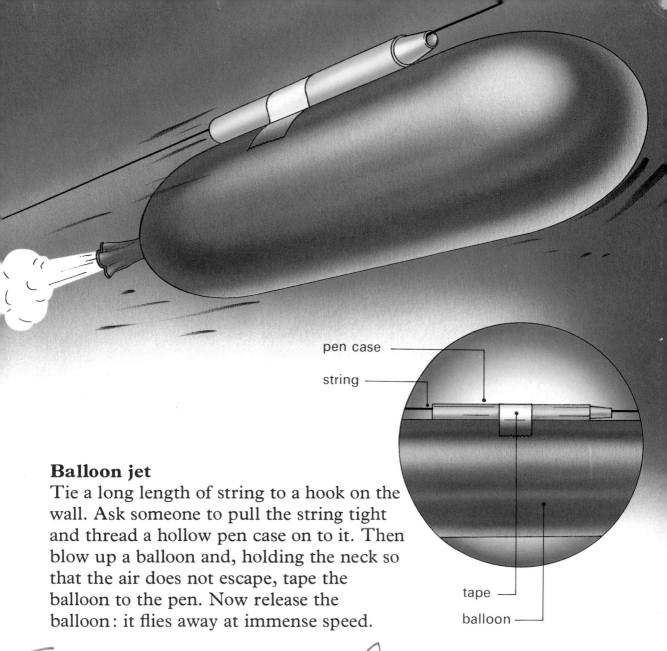

pen case

string

tape

balloon

Balloon jet

Tie a long length of string to a hook on the wall. Ask someone to pull the string tight and thread a hollow pen case on to it. Then blow up a balloon and, holding the neck so that the air does not escape, tape the balloon to the pen. Now release the balloon: it flies away at immense speed.

△ Tape a hollow pen case to the balloon while it is blown up. A sausage-shaped balloon works best.

✺ As the balloon deflates, it forces air out of the neck of the balloon. The air produces a reaction force that pushes the balloon forward. Jet and rocket engines work in a similar way. They heat air or gas and force it from the exhaust so that the reaction pushes the engine forward.

Motors on the move

Make two simple motors to see how energy can be changed into movement.

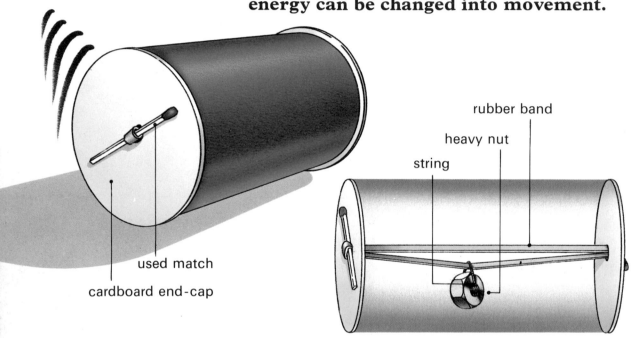

used match

cardboard end-cap

rubber band

heavy nut

string

△ Tie the nut to the rubber band first, and make sure it hangs loose. Next fix the band to one of the end-caps and place it in the tube with the end-cap in position. Then pull the band out of the tube and fix it to the other end-cap. Try making two rollers and racing them.

Returning roller
Take a tin can or empty detergent bottle and remove both ends to make a tube. Cut two circles in stiff card the same size as the tube, and pierce small holes in the middle of each one. Next, attach a weight to a strong rubber band and fix the band between the card circles inside the tube as shown. Now roll the tube across the floor and it will roll back to you; it's impossible to get rid of it!

As the roller turns, the rubber band twists because the weight stops it from turning too. This twisting stores energy in the band. When the roller is released, the stored energy is changed back into movement as the band untwists. Clockwork motors work like this. Many kinds of machines, including cars, contain their own stores of energy to change into movement.

Water motor

Take a tin can, remove the lid and make two small holes on opposite sides of the can near the base. Push two short straws into the holes so that they point away from the can as shown. Seal the joins with modeling clay to make them watertight. Suspend the can from a length of thread and place it over the sink. Keep on pouring water into the can from a jug. Watch the can spin round as water empties through the straws.

This motor works by action and reaction. As the water streams in jets from the can, it pushes against the can and turns it. The motor must be fed with energy in the form of falling water to keep turning. Many machines, such as electric trains, need to be supplied with energy to work.

△ Cars have their own energy supply in the form of fuel, whereas electric trains need to be supplied with energy in the form of electricity.

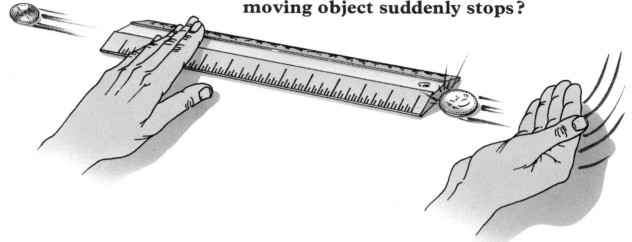

Where does the energy go when a moving object suddenly stops?

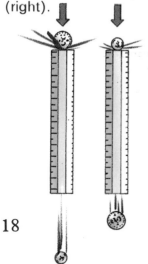

▽ The energy in the coins depends on their weight and speed. A large coin transfers more energy, making a small coin move fast (left). A small coin has less energy, causing a large coin to move slowly (right).

Stop-go

Take a long ruler and two coins, one large and one small. Hold the ruler firmly on a smooth tabletop with one hand, and place the small coin against one end of the ruler. Now slide the large coin along the tabletop so that it strikes the other end of the ruler. Even though the ruler cannot move, the small coin flies away from the end. Switch the coins and try other coins.

✳ The coin that strikes the ruler produces a force which travels through the ruler and gives the other coin a kick. In this way, the energy in the first coin is transferred to the second coin.

18

Upright matchbox

Take a closed matchbox full of matches. Challenge some friends to drop it from a height of about 10 in on to a smooth tabletop so that the box lands upright on one end. The box bounces every time and falls over. When you try, open the matchbox first. Make sure that it lands straight, and it will stay upright!

The matchbox normally bounces because it cannot lose all its energy and has to keep on moving. But when it lands open, only the inner tray keeps on moving. Friction quickly brings it to a stop, so that the box does not bounce.

△ Energy always has to go somewhere when objects collide; it cannot disappear. If one of the objects is fixed, then either the moving one bounces or one or both of the objects changes in shape. A change in shape causes friction, which takes up the energy by turning it into heat.

Reluctant movers

Everything has inertia, making it reluctant to move—and to stop.

△ Place the card so that one end protrudes about $\frac{1}{2}$ in over the edge. Try this trick out first so that you get to know how hard to flick the card.

The immobile coin

Place three coins on a smooth tabletop as shown, and put a playing card under the middle one. Challenge a friend to move the card without disturbing the coin. You can do it by giving the card a hard flick with a finger. It will fly out from under the coin without moving the coin at all!

A heavy object has more inertia than a light one. This means that the heavier something is, the more force is needed to get it moving. The card is very light, so it moves quickly when flicked. But the coin is too heavy to start moving and stays where it is.

Egg expert

Take two identical fresh eggs and hardboil one. Tell your friends that you can tell which egg is which. To identify them, spin each egg in a saucer, then touch the egg to stop it moving and let go. The hardboiled egg is easy to spin and stops immediately. But the fresh egg is hard to get spinning and it starts moving again after you have stopped it!

The yolk inside a fresh egg floats in the liquid white. Inertia makes the yolk revolve slowly when the shell is spun, and this slows the shell. But the yolk carries on turning when the shell is stopped, causing the egg to start spinning again when released. The hardboiled egg behaves differently because the yolk is held tight in the solid white inside the shell.

△ You hardboil an egg by boiling it for six minutes. Then leave it to cool or place it in cold water for a few minutes.

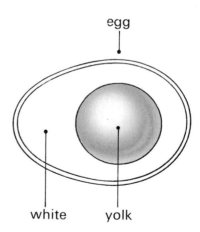

egg

white   yolk

21

To and fro

A little pull or push at the right time can really get things moving.

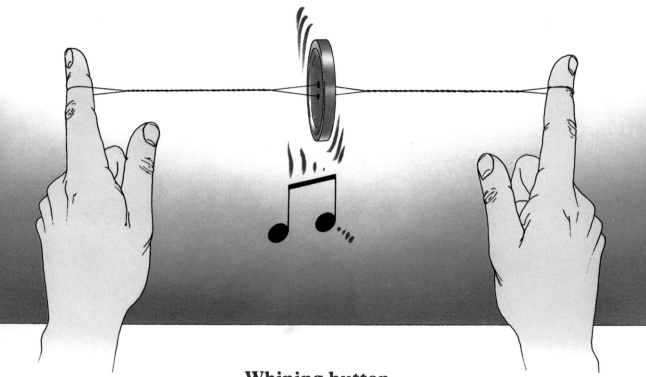

△ The button spins so quickly that it sets the air around it vibrating fast enough to give out a sound.

Whining button

Take a large button. Thread about a yard of thin but strong twine through it in a loop. Now hold the loop as shown, and wind up the twine by swinging the button in a circle. Pull the twine taut, and the button starts turning very quickly. If you then release and pull the twine at the right moments, you can get the button to rotate to and fro so fast that it makes a whine.

The twine takes a certain time to wind and unwind. If you release and pull on it in time with the winding and unwinding, you help to make the button turn faster. But if you release or pull at other times, you work against the movement and the button will slow down and stop.

Swingtime

Take five large bolts and suspend them from a line on different lengths of string as shown. Now hang a heavy object by a piece of string equal in length to that of one of the bolts and swing it. This bolt starts to swing much more than the others, but the heavy object slows. Then the object begins to speed up again and the swinging bolt slows down!

Each bolt is a pendulum and swings to and fro in a different time, depending on the length of its string. The swing of the heavy object is carried along the line and strings to the other bolts, and gives them a push to start them moving. If a bolt swings in the same time as the object, then a push will always come at the right time to build up the swing. If not, the push prevents a build-up so the other bolts move much less.

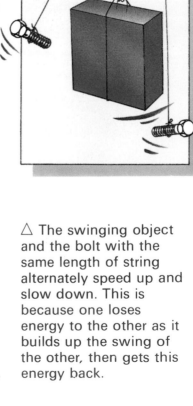

△ The swinging object and the bolt with the same length of string alternately speed up and slow down. This is because one loses energy to the other as it builds up the swing of the other, then gets this energy back.

Round and round

Experience the strange forces produced by circular motion.

△ Like the water in the bucket, you are pushed by centrifugal force in a vehicle as it turns. In fairground rides that go upside-down, the force keeps you in the car.

Whirling water

Take a plastic bucket and half fill it with water. Holding it by the handle, whirl the bucket in a circle. The water stays in the bucket, even when it is upside-down, as long as it is moving quickly.

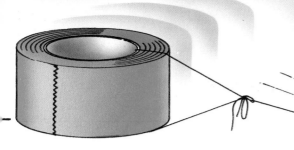

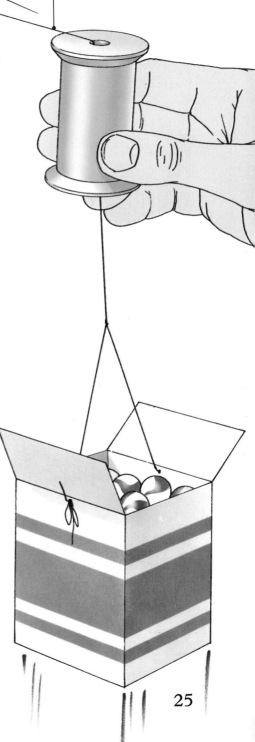

Replace the string if the reel begins to cut through it.

✳ As you whirl the bucket, you make two forces push and pull on it. The bucket and water try to fly away from you with a force called centrifugal force, while you pull on the handle with an equal centripetal force to keep the bucket moving in a circle. The water is pushed into the bucket by the centrifugal force, which is strong enough to overcome gravity.

Centrifugal lifter
Cut a piece of string as long as the distance from your hand to your elbow. Thread it through a cotton reel, and firmly attach a light object such as a reel of tape to one end and the carton shown on page 9 to the other end. With this device, you can raise weights placed in the carton without touching it. Whirl the object and it lifts the carton into the air.

✳ The force of gravity on the weights balances the centrifugal force of the object. As the object whirls faster, the centrifugal force increases and lifts the weights. Note that the force also depends on the length of string. As the object moves out from the reel, it circles less quickly to support the weights.

Continued *overleaf*

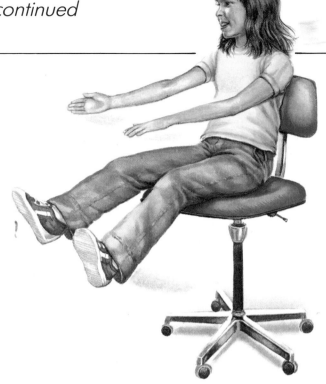

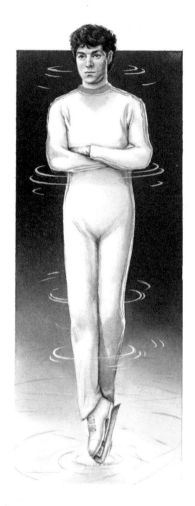

△ Skaters tuck in their arms to twirl quickly on the ice. In the same way, you can use your legs to change speed when you spin on a chair.

Spin fast, spin slow

Sit in a revolving chair and push your legs out straight. Then get a friend to spin the chair as fast as they can. As you turn, tuck your legs in. You suddenly begin to spin faster without any help. Now stick your legs out and you slow down.

✳ If you spin an object, the speed at which it will rotate depends on its diameter. The smaller its diameter, the faster it will spin. When you tuck your legs in, you reduce your diameter. The chair therefore speeds up. It slows down when you stick your legs out because you increase your diameter.

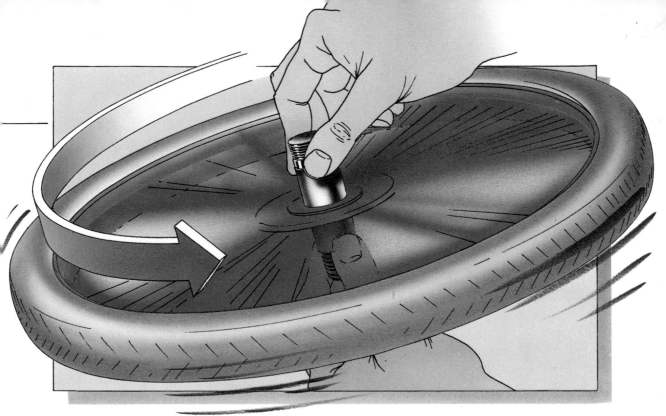

Crazy wheel

Hold a bicycle wheel upright in both hands, and start the wheel spinning with your thumbs. Now try to turn the wheel to the right or left. It twists in your hands to spin on its side. Try again but this time turn the wheel on its side. It now twists to the left or right.

✳ Turning the axle or axis of a spinning object makes the axle move at right-angles to the direction in which you turn it. This movement is called precession. It enables you to balance on a bicycle. If you begin to tilt to one side, you instinctively move the handlebars to turn the axle of the wheel in the same direction. Precession occurs and the wheel moves upright.

△ Use the front wheel of a bicycle and loosen the nuts on the axle to remove it from the forks. Be sure to tighten the nuts firmly when you put the wheel back.

Gyroscopes

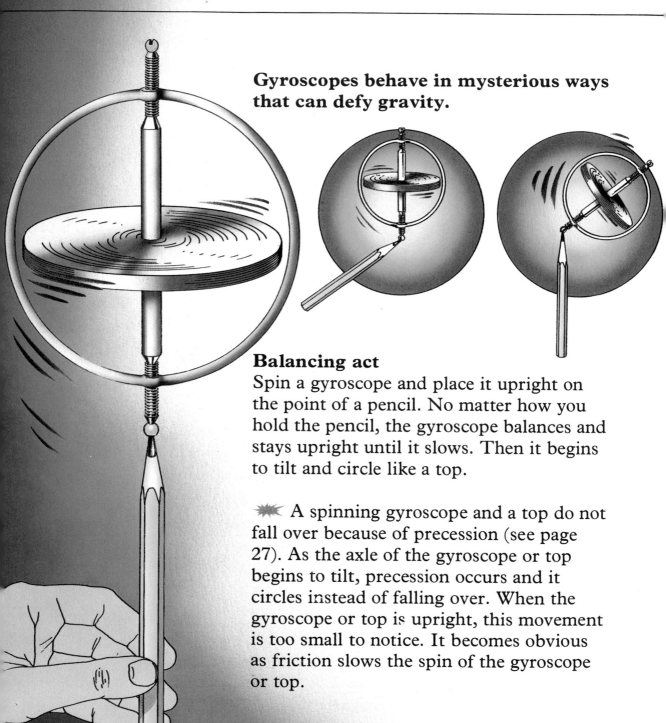

Gyroscopes behave in mysterious ways that can defy gravity.

Balancing act

Spin a gyroscope and place it upright on the point of a pencil. No matter how you hold the pencil, the gyroscope balances and stays upright until it slows. Then it begins to tilt and circle like a top.

A spinning gyroscope and a top do not fall over because of precession (see page 27). As the axle of the gyroscope or top begins to tilt, precession occurs and it circles instead of falling over. When the gyroscope or top is upright, this movement is too small to notice. It becomes obvious as friction slows the spin of the gyroscope or top.

Mystery force

Tie a piece of string to one end of the axle of a gyroscope and fix a hook to the other end as shown. Place a small object such as a nut on the hook. Now spin the gyroscope. Hold it horizontal and suspend it from the string. Release the gyroscope and it remains horizontal, circling gently as it supports the object.

✳ A horizontal gyroscope can support its own weight and the weight of an object attached to it if it spins fast enough. Gravity causes precession and the gyroscope circles. No one can explain why it can defy gravity and support itself in this way.

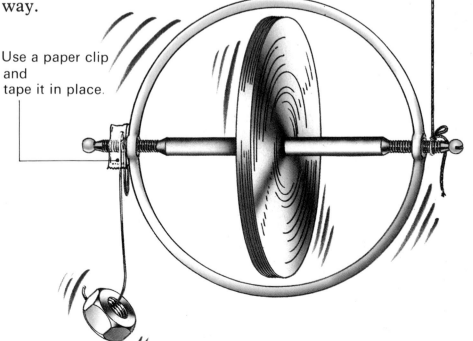

Use a paper clip and tape it in place.

29

More about movement

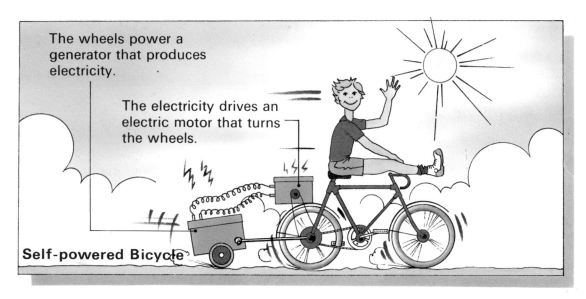

The wheels power a generator that produces electricity.

The electricity drives an electric motor that turns the wheels.

Self-powered Bicycle

△ Once it got going, would this self-powered bicycle work without any more pedaling? Unfortunately, it could not. Like all designs for perpetual-motion machines, friction would always take away its energy, making it slow down and stop.

Acceleration
When an object accelerates, its speed increases all the time, and it gets faster and faster. This happens if a force keeps pushing or pulling on an object, like gravity does when something falls to the ground.

Energy
When anything moves, it has a kind of energy called kinetic energy. The more it weighs and the faster it moves, the more energy it has. The moving object gets this energy as a force starts

it moving or makes it move faster.

Force
A force is the push or pull that is needed to make something start moving. Force is then required to make the object move faster, or to make it slow down and stop.

Friction
Friction is a force that occurs whenever anything on Earth moves. It makes moving objects slow down and may cause them to stop. Friction is produced

when the surface of one object moves over the surface of another. More friction is given if one object presses harder on the other. Brakes work by friction. As the brake presses harder on the wheel, more friction is produced and the vehicle slows down more quickly. Friction also occurs when objects move through the air or a liquid such as water.

Only in space is there no friction. This is because there is no air in space to cause friction. Satellites can therefore orbit the Earth without stopping.

Gravity

The Earth's force of gravity pulls objects to the ground so that their speed increases by nearly 32 feet per second for every second they fall. After falling for a second, the speed is 32 ft/s, after two seconds it is 64 ft/s and so on.

▽ When you go down a slide, a slight push or gravity gives the force to get you moving at the top. Then the force of gravity makes you accelerate down the slide. Finally, the force of friction makes you slow down and stop at the end.

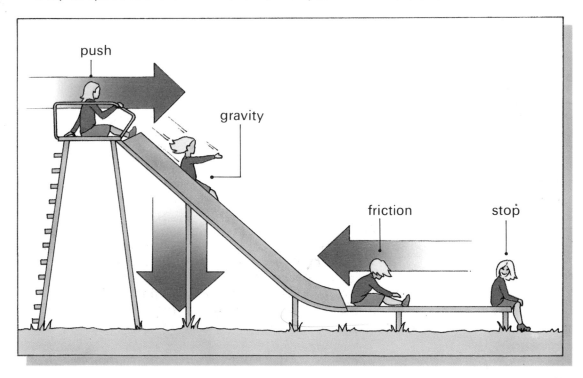
push

gravity

friction

stop

Index

PRINTED IN BELGIUM BY

proost
INTERNATIONAL BOOK PRODUCTION